RECONCILIATION THROUGH CONVERSATION

A PlayBook on Confronting Differences and the Advantages of Asking Uncomfortable Questions

DOMINIQUE KENNEDY

Yves Publishing, LLC

CONTENTS

Reconciliation Through Conversation:	v
About the Author	vii
Introduction	ix
1. Lost in Translation	1
2. He Said, She Said	3
3. Codeswitching, Colloquialisms, Jargon, Slang	5
4. Cultural & Linguistic Diversity	7
5. Screen-Free Reality or All the Tea	9
6. Stating No Without Actually Ever Saying No	11
Afterword	13
Suggested Reading & Listening	15
Also by Dominique Kennedy	17

RECONCILIATION THROUGH CONVERSATION:
A PLAYBOOK ON CONFRONTING DIFFERENCES AND THE ADVANTAGES OF ASKING UNCOMFORTABLE QUESTIONS

ABOUT THE AUTHOR

 Dominique Kennedy is an experienced and certified Speech-Language Pathologist. Dominique earned a bachelor's degree and master's degree in Communication Sciences and Disorders with an emphasis in Speech-Language Pathology. Her experience across settings includes schools, hospitals, rehabilitation centers, and early intervention. Through her private practice, she serves children and adults. She is a member of the American Speech-Language-Hearing Association (ASHA) and Special Interest Groups (SIGs) Fluency & Fluency Disorders and Augmentative & Alternative Communication. Through her desire to empower families, she has developed educational programs and resources. Dominique lives in the Atlanta Metro area of Georgia with her husband and their two daughters. She enjoys fine arts, music, and culture.

The information and advice contained in this book are based upon the research, and the personal and professional experiences of the author. They are not intended as a substitute for consulting with a healthcare professional. The publisher and author are not responsible for any adverse effects or consequences resulting from the use of any of the suggestions, preparations, or procedures discussed in this book. All matters pertaining to your physical health should be supervised by a healthcare professional. It is a sign of wisdom, not cowardice, to seek a second or third opinion.

Copyright © 2020 by Dominique Kennedy

All rights reserved. No part of this publication may be reproduced, scanned, uploaded, stored in a retrieval system, or transmitted, in any form or by any means, electronic, mechanical, photocopying, recording, or otherwise, without the prior written permission of the publisher.

ISBN: 978-1-7348653-3-2

INTRODUCTION

Perfection is not the goal but constantly growing in wisdom & understanding is.

As an avid reader, I've relentlessly sought out knowledge on various topics. I've always loved to read and write, beginning when I was much younger, because it was my way of seeking answers to the endless questions that persistently consumed my mind. My mother has scores of papers and essays and stories about my high interests, revealing a love for all things literacy, while detailing my insatiable appetite to know why. Which, by the way, has borderline gotten me in a precarious situation (i.e., disciplined) a few times, being that I didn't always know "when to stop" asking why.

I do recall my love for words as a child as I was the kind of kid that read the dictionary for sport. I remember being the first to anxiously put pen to paper in my second-grade class, just to get the coveted star or sticker on my creative writing piece, from my teacher, which I wore like a badge of honor. I also recall the feeling of bliss that came over me when I'd see that my written work earned a spot on the class bulletin board. Believe it or not, I still have my green marble notebook from my 7th grade English class (yes, intact & surprisingly legible). While some classmates grumbled and muttered about the English rules we were expected to learn and commit to memory, along with the copious notes that we were expected to keep in my middle school English class, I marveled at every concept that was introduced and each new lesson that unfolded in that class. I must have liked it because, to be honest with you, my penmanship is not my most exceptional quality, but when I look at that notebook, in particular, I can tell it was a prized possession for that eleven-year-old young girl.

Thankfully, these qualities have served me well in my profession both as a Speech-Language Pathologist and a "newish" author (of a total of four books in four months). As an unreformed relentless questioner, I revel in the regular questions that I get asked about 'what to do' and 'how it could be done' regarding speech and language strategies and techniques. It seems that everything that surmounts to a breakdown of the systems is often considered as a job for the communication professional. Whether it be a student struggling in school, a parent desperately wanting to be on the same page with their teen or a companion desiring to come to a compromise with their partner; many times, it's the communication professional that is sought out for the answers and solutions.

As a result, I have had the privilege of exercising my problem-solving muscle and wearing my thinking cap, as asking the right questions can, in many cases, lead to unlikely outcomes. It is through this pondering and through these conversations that breakthroughs can occur. Perhaps a breakthrough of the mind and thinking on a particular topic or thoughts of a specific person. Perhaps a breakthrough in the perception of a specific skill or ability. These outcomes serve as a springboard or bridge to gaining understanding.

Several circumstances can, at any given moment, serve to unite us or divide us. We must challenge ourselves to use the tools available to us to become better informed so that we can apply that knowledge to make well-informed decisions. This book provides sage suggestions that encourage communicators to think long and hard before deciding to place a valuation on or making presumptions about a communication partner. I hope that this book initiates internal dialogue and promotes positive external exchange.

CHAPTER 1
LOST IN TRANSLATION
WHAT IF WE CAN'T UNDERSTAND EACH OTHER

So, what if we can't understand each other? How do we navigate these differences?

Assess: We must first examine what we are seeking through this exchange. We must also assess what we can gain from one another.

Ask: What is my role in this exchange? Challenge within yourself, upon entering this conversation, what is it that I think I know about the other person? What "background noise' or experiences influence or shape my thoughts of self, my thoughts about you, or my viewpoints regarding me in relating to you?

Consider: What do I know about this type or style of communicative exchange? Are there any social norms or social rules that I need to be aware of? Are there things that I have been taught that I reference, or is there something that I must be taught to gain full access to this level of exchange? Have I asked the right questions? Have I provided clear enough, accurate information?

Apply: Determine what tools are available to aid in gaining understanding.

CHAPTER 2
HE SAID, SHE SAID
WHAT IF WE CAN'T COMMUNICATE CLEARLY

So, what if we can't communicate clearly? How do we navigate these differences in communication style?

Assess: We must first examine what we are seeking through this exchange. We must also assess what we can gain from one another.

Ask: What is my role in this exchange? Challenge yourself on what is it that I look forward to when entering this exchange & what gives me pause about having this conversation? What it is that I want you to see or understand & what reasonable take away is essential to the exchange.

Consider: What has worked during this exchange, and what should I eliminate what doesn't.

Are there ways to get to the root of what's problematic to cultivate a more productive interaction? Are there opportunities for me to take the lead, or should I follow their lead on positive and productive relationship building practices? Have I asked the right questions? Have I provided clear enough, accurate information?

Apply: Determine what resources and supports are needed to establish & facilitate healthful dialogue & exchange.

CHAPTER 3
CODESWITCHING, COLLOQUIALISMS, JARGON, SLANG
WHAT IF I JUST DON'T GET IT

So what if I just don't get it? How do we navigate these differences?

ASSESS: WE MUST FIRST EXAMINE WHAT WE ARE seeking through this exchange. We must also assess what we can gain from one another.

Ask: What is my role in this exchange? Challenge yourself on what is it that I consider the "gold standard" and what is it that I have created as an expectation from this person? What personal beliefs and values do I harbor regarding the differences in our communication style, and have I identified which may present as sources for conflict?

Consider: What have I done or committed to, in seeking more information to foster a meaningful exchange? Are there opportunities to acknowledge the individual's preference for terminology usage and conversation style while still honoring my own? Are there opportunities to determine what works and modify what doesn't per the interaction?

Have I asked the right questions? Have I provided clear enough, accurate information?

Apply: Determine the advantages and disadvantages of expanding a repertoire of speech knowledge as it relates to acknowledging differences in approach.

CHAPTER 4
CULTURAL & LINGUISTIC DIVERSITY
WHAT IF I DON'T KNOW WHAT TO SAY

So, what if I don't know what to say? How do we navigate these differences?

ASSESS: WE MUST FIRST EXAMINE WHAT WE ARE seeking through this exchange. We must also assess what we can gain from one another.

Ask: What is my role in this exchange? Challenge yourself on what is it that I have done to gain an understanding of this individual's culture and values? What influences my viewpoint and expectation of what I deem as appropriate or acceptable for this type of interaction with this individual in particular?

Consider: What have I done to facilitate a pleasant and productive exchange? Are there ways to acknowledge and celebrate our differences? Are there opportunities to have uncomfortable conversations while creating a safe space for the communicative exchange? Have I asked the right questions? Have I provided clear enough, accurate information?

Apply: Determine how to tailor interactions to honor the communication partners' values and cultural identity.

CHAPTER 5
SCREEN-FREE REALITY OR ALL THE TEA
WHAT IF I JUST DON'T CARE TO CARE

So, what if I just don't care to care? How do we navigate these differences?

Assess: We must first examine what we are seeking through this exchange. We must also assess what we can gain from one another.

Ask: What is my role in this exchange? Challenge yourself on what I have demonstrated and requested within this exchange & what my position is, on the matter. What knowledge base and observations impact my perspective on this topic, and what is a reasonable threshold?

Consider: What have I done to acknowledge or validate the perspective of the conversation partner? Are there opportunities to consider reinforcements or alternatives? Are there opportunities to compromise on potential outcomes? Have I asked the right questions? Have I provided clear enough, accurate information?

Apply: Determine how to best approach feeling connected to the people and experiences around you.

CHAPTER 6
STATING NO WITHOUT ACTUALLY EVER SAYING NO
WHAT IF I JUST DON'T WANT TO

So, what if I just don't want to? How do we navigate these differences?

ASSESS: WE MUST FIRST EXAMINE WHAT WE ARE seeking through this exchange. We must also assess what we can gain from one another (yes, even from a child).

Ask: What is my role in this exchange? Challenge yourself on what it is that you feel about the level of control being exhibited and sought in this exchange? What ideology guides my decision making regarding this dynamic and type of exchange?

Consider: What have I done to foster an environment that supports the individual's right to their position on the topic at hand? Are there opportunities for an agreement, or are we choosing to disagree respectfully? Are there opportunities to revisit this topic, or is it a closed case? Have I asked the right questions? Have I provided clear enough, accurate information?

Apply: Determine what message you are communicating through your actions, through your words or by your silence.

AFTERWORD

In all that we do, clear & effective communication is paramount. The desire to be seen & heard is one that is shared across culture, gender, age & class. But how do we get past our raging reality, or that which we deem is the most important point to be made in a given exchange, without demeaning, dishonoring, or dismissing the other party involved? Our charge is to ask questions--- of ourselves & of others, then allow answers to unfold. We must listen through uncompromised ears, and with a heart primed to receive, only then can the authentic conversation be had, and impending reconciliation occurs.

SUGGESTED READING & LISTENING

Chapman, Gary. 1992. The Five Love Languages.

Charity, Anne H., Mallinson, Christine. 2011. Understanding English Language Variation in U.S. Schools.

EP.#93: Dr. Shefali Tsabary: Conscious Parenting Can Change the World. Accessed July 14, 2020. https://www.youtube.com/watch?v=UXmkl3T77zE

Lippi-Green, Rosina. 1997. English with an Accent: Language Ideology and Discrimination in the United States.

Lythcott-Haims, Julie. 2016. How to Raise An Adult.

Maslow's Hierarchy of Needs. March 20, 2020. Accessed July 14, 2020. simplypsychology.org

Reaser, Jeffrey; Adger, Carolyn Tempe; Wolfram, Walt; Christian, Donna. 2017. Dialects at School: Education Linguistically Diverse Students.

Rubin, Gretchen. 2017. The Four Tendencies.

The 4 Stages of Cognitive Development. March 31, 2020. Accessed July 14, 2020. https://www.verywellmind.com/piagets-stages-of-cognitive-development-2795457

The Untethered Podcast. Episode 57: Cultural Sensitivity: Our Role as SLP's With Dominique Kennedy, MS, CCC-SLP. June 19, 2020. https://untetheredpodcast.com/2020/06/19/episode-57-cultural-sensitivity-our-role-as-slps-with-dominique-kennedy-ms-ccc-slp/

Unlocking Us With Brene' Brown. Brene with Ibram X Kendi on How to Be an Antiracist. Accessed on July 13, 2020. https://brenebrown.com/podcast/brene-with-ibram-x-kendi-on-how-to-be-an-antiracist/]

ALSO BY DOMINIQUE KENNEDY

Stuttering It's What You Think

Speech Culture

Speech Companion

www.ingramcontent.com/pod-product-compliance
Lightning Source LLC
Chambersburg PA
CBHW061349040426
42444CB00011B/3157